Bending the Light

Copyright © Patti Arsenault
Printed in Canada by Syntrak Print and Graphics
Graphic Design by Ruby Square Graphic Design
Cover painting by Bernadette Kernaghan, *A Portrait of Patti*

I would also like to give a shout out to my twin sis Cheryl and her husband Ken for several of the pics in the book. - Patti

Arsenault, Patti, 1964– , author
        Bending the Light: a journey into my soul
/ Patti Arsenault

ISBN 978-1-988395-20-3 (paperback)

Bending the Light

a journey into my soul

by Patti Arsenault

Secret Scrolls

When I was in high school I studied Ancient History. I was fascinated by ancient secret scrolls — the fact that they stood the test of time in their truth. I don't really believe that anyone owns the monopoly on truth but I do believe we each own our own truth. I have put my thoughts into quotes that I like to call my *Secret Scrolls* as they are my truth. They are scattered throughout the book as the thoughts scattered throughout my life.

> *Separate the thought that we perceive and discern with the eyes. These are illusions. Only the mind and the heart can perceive and discern. If the mind or the heart has been damaged or biased everything will be seen through this lens.*
> *It is called suffering. P*

Life Happens and when it happens you laugh, you cry, you get angry, you get hurt and there will be moments that bring you to your knees. This is a piece of my life and a piece of my heart which I very much wish to share with you. Take care of your hearts my friends. They are so very precious and so very worthy of life and love. Much love from my heart to yours.

I want to tell you a magical story... it is about the beautiful people I have had the great fortune of knowing on this Island. When the mass shooting happened at the First Baptist Church in Sutherland Springs, Texas, the feelings of helplessness were overwhelming.

I couldn't just sit by and do nothing. I contacted my Island friends and asked for their help to send a parcel of love to reach the hearts of those directly effected by this tragedy.

My Island friends responded immediately, and our parcel of love was sent out. I know it may sound crazy, but love can actually be put in a box in the mail. That night while I lay in bed, I said a prayer. "Please help the box of love to find the hearts of those in need." I said one more prayer before I closed my eyes that night. "Please, Universe, could you give me a sign that the love in the box will find its way?"

The next morning, I awoke. I let my dog Max out for his morning business. It had been a cold damp night. I looked down at my front step. The frost had formed this magical scene. A sign from the Universe! Love always finds its way.

we bend the light

The Butterfly House

Now for some magic about you and blue butterflies: blue butterflies have iridescent wings. Because of the size of the microstructure in the wings, they are the same wavelength as light and the layers in the wings react strongly to visible light. Bending of the light pattern of the wings results in their being blue. From my heart to yours my very first poem called *Rules and Requests for the Butterfly House*. My friends, I hope that each of you realizes that you bend the light.

we bend the light

Rules & Requests for The Butterfly House

Stay on the Stone pathway.
Do not step on the butterflies.
Do not touch or entrap.
Except it seemed
We were all entrapped
Blue Butterflies, people and me.
Locked up inside the four walls.
All prisoners.
Except there were no criminals here
Just iridescent wings layering their
Ancestral qualities through pure light.
Surviving those heavy rains that can kill.
Each raindrop that touched the wing
Turning into a
Spherical ball of water
Gathering the dirt along the way
Rolling off the wing
Cleansing the window
Bending the light once again.
Sometimes their wounds were evident.
The wingspan widening to reveal a gouged hole.
Yet still
They flew.
I seemed unnoticeable
But I had hoped they would seek me out.
I stayed very still.
Some fluttered but never lingered.
Sometimes three or four gathered around my shoulder
Discussing their query.
Then I noticed Him and Her.

They were old.
He walked with a walker.
She held his arm with both of hers.
She was weak
But her Man had a walker and between the walker and his legs
They both stood.
He would shift his gaze and his weight appropriately
For Her.
And then a Blue Butterfly would appear.
Ripened fruit seemed to attract their interest.
What silent communication they displayed
Appeared to support her smile.
A camera was around his neck.
When she sat
He took pictures.
They smiled at each other.
She became suddenly flustered.
Fear and confusion registered on her face.
He noticed.
It was time to leave.
It was rushed.
They took up too much space.
He tried to maneuver.
The door was heavy.
He let go
Of Her.
She began to fall.
My legs were fast and moved before I thought.
I caught her before she fell to the ground.
A Blue Butterfly became engulfed in the activity.
The door closed harshly behind us.
We were now all in the atrium

The old man, his woman, the Blue Butterfly and me.
The old man let go of his walker
And embraced his woman.
Her head rested on his shoulder.
They smiled at me
And left.
The Blue Butterfly was on the ground.
The ripened fruit still lingered on my fingertips
And seemed to attract its attention.
The Blue Butterfly glided up to my shoulder
And widened its full wingspan.
Be Still.
This is life.
See you next season.
Oh, there is one last Request before you leave.
Check yourself in the mirror
For "hitchhikers."

we bend the light

For me compassion is the strongest of all human energies. It is the seed that can surpass fear, hatred, and ignorance. Our light can shine on this seed and cause growth. I choose the color blue as it is the highest frequency visible light. The higher the frequency, the faster the oscillations and thus the higher the energy. The highest-frequency ultra-violet light (or the lowest wavelength) is violet. However, the highest-frequency visible light to the human eye is **blue.** The world could use a lot of blue right now!

we held the light

A screen sits in a window. What is on the other side. What do you see? Do you see it clearly? What side of the window are you on? Are you on the inside looking out or the outside looking in? Remove the window. Remove the screen. That is reality. P

Junkie

The word was said
And written Junk
It meant useless
Or of little value
Waste
Trash
Debris
I saw a person on the ground
With a sign
A passerby said the word Junk
But added ie
I wanted to be Charlotte
And spin my web
With the word "Treasure"
Instead
And set them both free.

The Family Reunion

Every year my parents get asked to go to the Stewart family reunion requested by a distant relative that they have never met. Each year they decline but this year they decided to go. Since I have no life I asked if I could tag along. I did ask my twin sister if she would care to accompany us, but she had other plans. Of course, she did, as she has a life and apparently at age 45 I do not. Here we are trucking along, my parents in the front seat and me sitting all by myself in the back seat. I feel 12 again. Clearly the "L" on my forehead doesn't stand for Lucky. I start thinking about the twin and near as I can figure the closest thing I come to an identical twin is an alien cloning experiment gone horribly wrong.

As I look out the window of the car, I realize we must be nearing our destination. It was hard to tell though if we were at the right spot. The whole area was covered with old abandoned travel trailers and one decrepit school bus. In the center of all this looked like a shack with a huge chimney spewing out fire. It sure looked a little shady to me. The first to greet us was Joe, a great big burly fellow, about six foot two, close to 300 lbs, wearing an undersized undershirt, belly showing, unshaven and wreaking of alcohol. He said, "You folks must be here to see Momma; looks like she lured another family." You know I don't really care for the word lured! It somehow sounded sinister. Now don't get me wrong, "Momma" was a lovely person and she was very informative but three hours later and it was long past the time we should be leaving. Time to take a breather.

Outside I went, gasping for fresh air. It suddenly donned on me that no one else had arrived for the "Big" reunion! Not a single solitary soul! Why, I wondered. I suddenly realized what had happened. All those abandoned travel trailers, all those distant relatives! They never left! They were probably buried alive in their little trailers, hundreds of them over the years! This explained a few things and made a clear decision for me. Back inside I went. I start talking out of the corner of my mouth, "Mom... let's... go... now." Finally, we are headed back home.

As soon as I arrived home the twin calls. I know she is feeling guilty and probably a little curious as to how my trip went. So, I am thinking to myself, "Man I'm pissed! A creepy, scary day from Hell and not a twin to be found! But then it dawns on me and I have a plan. An evil twisted plan. So, I reply to my sister "Oh my gosh, Sarah, it was great! I can't wait to tell you everything. See you in a few minutes."

I then don my best dress, put on some heels, bright red lipstick and some fancy jewels. I grab my digital camera, take a slew of pictures from a Georgian Mansion Design magazine, grab the husband and kids, and 15 minutes later I am at The Twin's.

I can see the expression on my twin's face. "Oh... don't you look nice," I know I have her hooked. The thing is, my twin is very attracted to the finer things in life.

So I say, "Yeah, I kind of had to dress for the occasion as the reunion required semi-formal dress and that isn't even the half of it!"

I can see the look on her pathetic looking face and it's a look of pure envy. "The Stewarts were such good hostesses and our every whim was catered to, including exquisite fine dining with our second cousins Cassandra and Melanie, who invited us to stay for a few weeks during the summer."

My husband is standing nearby, and I pretend like I have to go hug him, but actually I have to bury my face in his chest for fear of disclosing my spasms of pure stifled laughter. But the best part is coming up. I tear myself from my husband and plunk myself back down beside the twin. And there it comes: a picture of a grand master bedroom unrivaled in its magnificence, and atop the huge canopied bed was an antique painting perhaps 200 years old of a very beautiful blonde Victorian lady.

I say to my twin, "That's our great-great-great-great grandmother. Isn't she beautiful?"

My twin says, "Oh, my God, Kate, she is beautiful! Oh my God, she looks just like us!"

I can no longer keep it inside and laughter pours out of me. Uncontrollable laughter. Laughter that hurts your stomach and tears pour down my face.

It was then my twin says, "What's wrong?"

And I say, "You've been HAD!"

Alas, life does seem a little more fulfilling lately!

One could say that the first step to attaining our wishes is to envision them, the next to embody them, and finally the joy of knowing you will have the strength to see them through. P

Car Troubles

On the off chance you haven't met me before, I can tend to be a little OCD, which basically means I like certain things a lot and when I like them a lot, I use them a lot! So, when my husband suggested we take an alternative route home... I thought nah, I like my favourite road! But then he stated that the instructor at our course tonight suggested that perhaps the Blue Shank might not be the best road to take given the road conditions. Sooo, being a good student we took an alternative route.

Not even five minutes into our alternate route, flashing red lights appear behind us. Of course, being the good citizens we are, we thought this could not possibly be for us! But alas it was, and being the good citizens we are, we pulled over!

When I say we, it is not to say that both of us are driving, but that I am a backseat driver in the front seat! Now just to bring you all up to speed, our car is in the shop and we have a loaner car! The police officer is now getting out of his car... I am searching for registration and insurance and cannot find anything.... I am like, ohhhh nooo, we are in so much trouble!

Police officer then states, "Do you know why I pulled you over?" "No sir, we do not" we replied. "Well, you hit a pot hole and your hubcap fell off and I wanted to put it back on!" He did so, high-fived me and went on his way!

Being 50+

Shoppers Drug Mart at 8:50: I am picking up a few last-minute items, get to the cash, and decide, what the heck, I will get a scratch ticket. Now I know you're gonna think I must have won the jackpot or why else would I post this story, but nope, that's not it.

The cashier is ringing through my items and then I ask for the scratch ticket... long pause... then the words "CAN I SEE YOUR ID?"

It took a few moments for this to register in my brain, 'cause you know the whole "I am getting up there" kinda grandma brain where it takes a while for things to sink in, but when it did... I can't quite remember how the whole thing went down, but I believe I jumped over the counter, tossed her up in the air, hugged her, and left whistling!

As we grow older and "wiser" we are better able to read a person. It then becomes second nature to be able to "read them like a book." Now replace the word "read" with "judge!" This is our reality. P

Busy Days

It began almost like any other Friday in Patti's life. But this was an extra special Friday... for Patti knew that her grandson was coming today, and there were many preparations.

Mr. Dylan's room was all prepared and the cookies were all baked. When he finally arrived, he jumped straight into her arms, kissed her on the cheek and said, "I missed you Nana." But that was only the beginning, then off to her brother-in-law's birthday party... loads of family, chocolate cheesecake, and maybe a story or two!

Well, as per usual, her Fridays also included cleaning the clinic. It had been a long day, and Grampy took Mr. Dylan home while Nana cleaned. She cleaned until 9:00 pm, then got in her car and headed home. She was so tired, she did not realize that the police were trying to pull her over.

When she finally pulled over... she knew she had done something wrong... what had it been? Maybe she had forgotten to stop at the stop sign. Was she speeding? (probably not if you know Patti at all) But who knows, she was very tired.

The police officer was kind but to the point, did a few routine questions, then said, "Do you know why I pulled you over Ma'am?" But Patti, as tired as she was, told him she was not sure. Then with a twinkle in his eye, he said, "You forgot to put your lights on and we just wanted to make sure you were OK... here is a $10 gift card to Tim Hortons... have a Merry Xmas."

As Patti snuggles Mr. Dylan to sleep that night, she has only one thing on her mind. Thank you, Mr. Police Officer, whoever you are!

Twin Talk

Scene: Twin's kitchen: helping The Twin clean out the fridge so the compost bin can be put to the curb.

Twin One: Do you think I should throw out the jam?

Twin Two: What's the expiry date?

Twin One: September 2018.

Twin Two: Keep it.

Twin One: Why? What am I going to use it for?

Twin Two: Remember Girl Guides: "Hope for the best, prepare for the worst"

Twin One: What do you mean?

Twin Two: Zombie Apocalypse!

Twin One: More like Alien Invasion!

In Unison: Or both!

Twin One: What about the ketchup and mustard?

Twin Two: I could eat ketchup and mustard.

Twin One: Yeah, me too.

Just Another Day

My day kind of started like the Pink song, *So What:*

Na na na na na na, na na na na na na
Na na na na na na, na na na na na na
I guess I just lost my husband
I don't know where he went...

Not even kidding! My grandson and I dropped my husband and the dog off at the park. Two hours later, we still couldn't find them. All the while this crazy song is going through my head. Not to mention I just passed my UNLIMITED ACCESS TO MY HOUSE twin sister on the road driving her lovely Lincoln, waving politely and wearing my lovely dress! Guess it's just gonna be one of those days!

What would be the point of leaving Planet Earth to explore space if we haven't yet learned to properly communicate with an ant? P

Emergency!

I have discovered that sitting in "Emerg" can actually be an interesting experience. For one thing, your sister the nurse stops by to check on things. Sisters are awesome!

I also learned that people that sit next to you can be extraordinarily kind and considerate considering their leg may be broken. Not to mention a guy with a bandaged hand used his other hand to open the door for an elderly lady with a cane.

I also learned that there are a lot of Patricias that get injured on a Tuesday afternoon in the town of Summerside. Four in fact. What are the odds! Oh, and it turns out prioritizing patients in regards to severity is a good thing for anxiety ridden, overly dramatic, vertically challenged blondes, 'cause from my perspective, the long wait just means that I am not dying!

It turns out Patti has a bad burn! How do I know this? Well it turns out my doctor said so! And you know why I trust what my doctor says? It just so happens her name is Dr. Burns! And that, my friends, is how I spent a Tuesday afternoon in April!

Trust

My daily ritual of walking.

Sun shining. A nice breeze.

A large bird swoops down passing in front.

A warning. I continue.

Another large bird crosses my path.

Another warning. The young are near.

Protection. I continue with my walk.

A thought. No harm.

Trust.

Awake new day.

Late. Rushing.

Start vehicle.

Proceed too fast.

Memory. The young are near.

Slow down.

Small. Vulnerable. In sight.

Parents guiding.

A thought. No harm.

I stop.

Delicate crossing.

Parents follow.

Trust.

The Great Birds

I watched the great birds swirling around the church steeple
which was positioned in the valley between the hills.
A battle had ensued for the highest point to perch.
Each bird dived at the other fighting for victory
Slowly moving away from the steeple
Only to be consumed by a war in the distant skies.
A small sparrow came fluttering gently in
to rest upon the ledge of the window of the church
where the sun angled its rays.

we hold the light

Namaste

What gives anyone the right to decide who and what we are
As if they were there watching us
Seeing our thoughts throughout infancy, childhood, the teens,
and adulthood.
Struggling to speak
Using only the words outside
How could anything outside of us know what is in
How is that even possible to explain
As if there could possibly be a chance
For even ourselves to understand each moment
Every thought
Every experience
Every joy
Every heartache
No more could we explain each other than the other to explain us
Not even our thoughts define us
So, when we pass each other
During our time
Know
That is the truth for all beings
And greet each other with recognition and love
Namaste.

*I've heard it said so many times —"It is what it is"
— But what if it's not? What if it isn't what it isn't?
What if it never was what it was? What if it will never
be what it will be? Then does that still make it what it
is? Doesn't that still mean "It is what it is ?" P*

> *An undisciplined mind is like having a double-edged sword in an untrained hand... wounding yourself and others. P*

Dear Friend

The decorations are all put away. Strange how one memory lingers in my mind. It was a few weeks until Christmas. I was talking on my cell and completely distracted with Christmas shopping in the Mall. I saw him out of the corner of my eye and felt my heart tighten.

Time seemed to slow down. He was walking with a walker and appeared bruised, as if he had been through some terrible accident. When I approached, his face lit up with that same sweet twinkle in his eye.

I remember how many times over the past few years he had been there for me. The visits to my office, "Just dropping by to see if you could spare a few moments for an old fella!" Indeed, he was the highlight of those days! I recall a rather challenging day in my personal life and having to stop in the mall to pick up a card. I was up at the cash when I heard this familiar voice saying, "Would you be able to spare a few moments for an old fella?" As if the universe devised a plot for us to meet and there he would be sitting on the bench in the Mall. We sat and shared a piece of our lives. Before I left, he embraced me with his heart and eyes and said, "I love you," and that was enough.

Now I was looking up into a face that had given me so much. He shared the story of his accident. I couldn't imagine how someone could survive such a horrible incident, much less be standing there with the determination of a soul that truly wished to live life to the fullest.

He was much taller than me, and when I looked up and took in his whole appearance, I knew that nothing could shatter this man's spirit. He was wearing a red sweater and had a Christmas tie that lit up just like his eyes, and all I could think or even imagine is that he was Santa Claus. He was the true meaning of Christmas.

The Goodness remains, and he was sufficient despite changing external forces. His actions meant the world to me, and I was so much better for him being here. I touched his hand, and I could feel him loosen his grip on his walker. I knew that once again, the universe had conspired to reveal the true story of Christmas! Indeed, maybe, just maybe, the universe conspired to reveal what was truly important in life.

Beneath the Surface

Deep beneath the surface
She climbs up to the skies
And reaches to the highest branches
Where the stars touch the crown
And in so doing
The mercenary weeps her fears
Conquering the stem of her thoughts
And the richness of the soil that supports all life
Reveals the underground threads
Of all her existence
Weaving its intricate web
Into a moment of clarity
The unforeseen wakening her sleep
A weeping child
Staggering her trusting footsteps

Opening her eyes
There is no space
No vast cosmos
No Perfectly measured time
Travelled
Just two little girls sleeping under the stars
And darkness.

*Do we climb a tree to get to the top
or to expand our visual range? P*

we held the light

Rainbow Valley

Being an empty nester has its challenges, and when one of those challenging days appears, there are always the memories to reflect on. My son was finishing up Grade One when his teacher suggested a class trip to Rainbow Valley. When the school asked for volunteers, I jumped at the chance to spend the day with the kids, help chaperone and drop by an alien spacecraft! I was assigned to chaperone my son and a little girl that lived around the corner from us.

Now things would have been great had I not decided that I could maneuver a swan! Ten minutes out in the pond, and me and the kids got stuck in the mud. It wouldn't have seemed so bad had we not been so far from shore! So much for being Supermom! Not even my web shooters were working that day! Alas, with my head hung low, the rescuers came and brought us safely to shore.

Now the day was pushing along, and I noticed some apprehension on the little girl's face when we were approaching the Witch's Cave. Witch's caves aren't necessarily places I prefer to hang out. I am much more an Alien vs. Predator kind of a hero. But alas, this little girl with her big beautiful eyes was relying on me to see her through. You see, she really wanted to be brave like the other kids, and she came all prepared with a flashlight just in case!

I looked into her big eyes and said, "You see, this is my hand. I am going to place your hand in mine and not let go the whole time, and if you get scared, you just squeeze really tight and we will turn back." Her little face seemed to relax, and she placed her tiny little hand in mine.

Straight through the whole tour, she did not let go of my hand. The flashlight remained on, and even when the Witch came jumping out at her, she just simply looked at me with her big eyes and squeezed a little tighter on my hand. Many times, I asked if she wanted to turn back, and she said "No." Her brave little heart made me feel so proud of this little girl.

The day is nearing its end, and we have one last excursion — the rollercoaster! The whole time my son is just kind of tagging along and enjoying his day, but now I realize the closer we get, the more apprehensive he seems. We are just about to jump on board the rollercoaster when my son says, "Mom, I'm scared. I don't think I can do it." He was not budging.

This is when I realize that Rainbow Valley was the most magical place. The little girl with the big eyes went straight over to my son. She said, "Don't worry," as she placed her hand over his. "I won't let go the whole time, and if you get really scared, you can just squeeze really tight and close your eyes and I will be right here!"

we held the light

Healer

She had probably passed through that old creaky wooden door thousands of times. It never did close easily. She thought there were many similarities between her and the door. She felt old. She was old. It wasn't hard to tell by her appearance. Her long golden locks had turned to a more grayish dull color. Her joints creaked and her body seemed to need oiling these days. It wouldn't be long before she laid her head to rest. One of these days, but not quite yet. Besides, it wasn't so bad to think of death. She did not fear it. What was there to fear? She had done all she could. She had cared for her family, loved them, and protected them to the best of her ability. There was honor in that. There was freedom with that.

Most of her family had moved on. The boys were now men. Her boys — she missed them so much. They were coming home this very day! The whole family was coming! Oh, just to see them again and their extended families would be absolutely delightful. Funny how she still called them her boys now that they had grown into such fine men. There had been so many challenges! She used to think that nothing ever got better until you faced it, and sometimes the hardest thing to face was yourself. She glanced out the window, across the street, and saw the power lines. The memories came flooding in. Fourteen years seemed like a long time, but to her it was yesterday. She had tried so hard to show those boys how to live again after great tragedy.

The younger brother's name was Eli. The doctor said he was in the 50th percentile for height which basically meant he was little. But his heart seemed to make up for it, as it seemed to grow two sizes every day. He was just that kind of a kid. Every lost, broken, starving, lonely critter he came across he brought home. Some in his pocket, others in the back of his wagon. Most of them left better off for his acquaintance. Once he even brought home a snake. He was told to tend to that in the shed. Eli could make you smile simply by sitting next to you. Things changed though, after the tragedy. The night his father didn't return. Eli's heart simply seemed to be ripped apart. His soft gentle hands appeared to tremble over the slightest thing, and tears fell easily and silently from his bright blue eyes.

The older boy was named Jackson. He was much like his father in stature and strength. He was a little more headstrong, a capable athlete, friendly with a wide grin. You always felt safer when he was around. When he hugged you, he would pick you right up off the ground. Nobody ever really knew if he was afraid of anything. He would just give you that grin and jump right in, feet first… he was, after all, a natural descendant of a family of puck shooters and Zeppelinists. He never took himself too seriously, and was quick with his wit. He desperately grieved for his father and soon he too changed.

She had struggled with the challenges of helping to raise two lads that were as different as day and night. Both boys had lost something of themselves after the tragedy. Fear had crept into their lives and fear preyed on your weakness. Eli had become afraid of his own shadow. He no longer brought any critters home to tend to. She could see that the joy of being himself had left him. He spent most of his days doing little or nothing of value. At night she would sit with him. Sometimes he would awaken, sobbing uncontrollably. The tears absorbed into her long hair. She thought to herself that maybe she could absorb his pain as well. The sensitive one had lost his strength.

Jackson had tried hard to fill his father's shoes. He had become too overprotective, too controlling, not even giving himself time to come into his own. Jackson spent his days playing video games or hovering over his younger brother. They argued a lot. Jackson tried to control everything. He was constantly ordering his younger brother around. Fear was his constant companion. Jackson stopped doing his chores around the house; he no longer participated in the sports he loved so much. He would kick things around and lost his temper a lot. The strong one had lost his sensitivity.

She had seen them arguing again that day. The older one was taunting the younger one. He had the younger one's new shoes. He said, "You can't wear these. Are you crazy? Do you know what they will say?" To which Eli replied, "I don't care! Give them back or I'll tell!" Jackson was agitated and continued, "They will hurt you! You will get another black eye! There isn't a chance in hell, not a chance you're going to wear these!" And with that the older boy flew out the front door with the younger one trailing. "Try and get them now, you little dweeb!" But the younger one was not fast enough.

She was not fast enough. She heard the argument, heard it leave the house, heard it leave the yard, heard it trail across the street and she dashed straight out to the front yard after the both of them. When would they learn? Something had to change, or those two boys were never going to face themselves. There were unspoken words between the boys. Unspoken words were the most powerful because they were always the truth, and the truth can be the most difficult thing to face. Neither of the boys had grown enough to face this truth. She knew the truth. Her only hope was that both of the boys would have the courage to face it, and become the men they were meant to be. Now she was running around outside trying to help a situation that had gotten out of control. She was too late. Jackson still must have retained some of his athleticism because he threw those sneakers hard and high. There, up high on the power line, a pair of sneakers dangled. Those most precious sneakers the younger boy had painstakingly chosen for their flare, their curves, and their craftsmanship.

The older brother had gone too far. Eli hung his head ashamed of the tears that freely flowed down his face. It was over. She had started across the street, she couldn't change this. The damage was done. It had been her intention to stand between the boys to try to make it right like she always did. It was too late, too late for many reasons. Suddenly she was aware that she had stopped in the middle of the street! She did not see the car! The pain instantly hit her lower body! She collapsed, her golden locks cascading over the pavement.

She had a broken leg, a cast, a few cuts and bruises but, for all, was none the worse for her ordeal. Not so bad, all things considered. The boys had long since forgotten about the sneakers and their argument. For weeks the boys hardly left her side. She couldn't have been more pleased. Eli attended to her wounds. His hands, unsteady at first, seemed to know exactly what to do. It was like riding a bike. Eli hadn't forgotten, the love was still there, hidden, buried by fear. Jackson used his strength to carry her everywhere. For weeks he did so gently, lifting her about as if she weighed little or nothing, his strength returning like a lightning bolt. The brothers had become united in her recovery. Between the two boys, she had survived. Six weeks later, the cast came off. She retained a slight limp, otherwise things were back to normal in the household. A new normal — it was called acceptance.

Her thoughts returned to the present. The boys had arrived! She was waiting for them. Now both men were beside her. They gently lifted her into the car and travelled to the hospital. Eli and Jackson carefully took her in and placed her on the hospital bed. Never wavering in their attention to her — it was time. She could hear a lone barking dog in the distance. The dog had a very distinctive bark. It was the cry for a fallen comrade. There was no way she could repay the boys for their kindness. She had been an abandoned, starving, four-legged golden retriever the night the boys found her. She had wanted to repay that kindness. Both boys laid their hands on her. Eli then placed his strong, steady hand over his brother's. "I am sorry," he said. The sensitive one had gained back his strength. Tears flowed freely down Jackson's face. "Me too," he said. The strong one had gained back his sensitivity. Now it was done. She had completed her last task. The veterinarian placed the needle into her leg.

What does it mean to be in the dark?
It simply means we cannot see. P

Prison

Mind, heart, open, closed.
Prison, lock up, behind bars
No entry, no exit, walls.
Key, small piece,
Cut to fit
Turn inward
Unbolt, unlatch, unbar, unfasten
Open
Door unlocks.

Courage

I recall some odd years ago waiting impatiently in a doctor's office when in she walked. She noticed me immediately and came over to greet me as if there hadn't been thirty plus years since we had last spoken. Her eyes, despite the many lines around them, still held their sweet smile. That was the day Courage walked back into my life. To the outside world, she could give the appearance of someone who led a very hard life. It was true. Her life had tragic circumstances, and those memories that held her in their grip would be choked down with a smoke, a drink or whatever she chose to swallow, revealing to the world her pain. I, on the other hand, could give the outside appearance of someone who had it all put together. Not much got past Courage though, and for whatever reasons, she embraced me as her friend.

The thing about Courage was she kind of told it like she saw it. She definitely stood outside the box, and she was wholeheartedly truthful. The day she got the diagnosis that her cancer was terminal, she said to me, "Do you think it's wrong that I really don't mind to go?" This made me really sad, but I knew it was the truth and I guess I understood.

I work at the front desk in a busy clinic answering phones, waiting on patients and one of the calls I answered happened to be from Courage. She said, "You've got to help me! My daughter's really upset with me. She wants me to go in a coffin and I want to be cremated! What should I do?" Well, you couldn't beat around the bush with Courage, so I simply stated that since her daughter was the one who had to live with her decision, she should leave this up to her. She seemed satisfied with my answer and hung up.

Courage loved to sit out on her back deck. During the day, I would find her feeding the blue jays, and at night gazing up at the stars. I am not sure if it was her medications or the mere fact that she was terminal, but there were many nights she could not sleep, and that is where I would find her. I would sit with her sometimes, gazing up at the vast darkness and marveling along with her about the mysteries that lay beyond Planet Earth.

I wanted to do something special for Courage, so I called some friends from the astronomy club and arranged for us to do some real stargazing. The astronomy guys took us out to an open field with their big telescope showing us wonders we had never seen before. Our absolute favorite stars were what the astronomy guys called Albireo A and Albireo B from the constellation Cygnus, the Swan. To the naked eye, they appeared to be only one star, but through a telescope they were actually the most beautiful double stars, with one shining brightly in gold and the other in blue-green. What fascinated us was that the double stars could remain so close together and yet not cause each other to burn out. The astronomy guys explained that it appeared the center of mass was probably between them, and not inside them, which allowed the smaller blue green to orbit the larger gold one. The night was getting on, and I knew Courage was getting tired, so it wasn't long before we were saying goodnight in her front doorway. Our evening had been magical. I still remember Courage's words and the tears I shed over them, "You know, someday, God willing, he will place us up in the sky as stars side-by-side to shine for all eternity."

It wasn't long before Courage ended up in the hospital. The thing that surprised her so much was that her room was always full of visitors from every walk of life. One night, long past visiting hours, I still sat in her room. It was difficult to leave at this stage. Courage looked at me with such clarity, her lower lip quivering and said, "You know, had I known how loved I was, I wouldn't have made the choices I made in life but now it's too late." The tears spilled down my face. Then in the same breath with her chin up, she said, "I have decided I don't believe in death. Why is it we never question such a useless fact? There is no such thing as non-existence. Someday I will show you. She had also decided that waiting for death in her bed was not her thing, and made arrangements to get passes from palliative care so she could attend a few of those kitchen parties she loved so much. Courage was late returning to palliative care one evening, much to the nurse's concern, to which Courage replied, "Yes, I am quite aware I am supposed to be dying in my bed like everyone else around here. I simply do not wish to wait for death. It will come when it comes!"

The cancer had become so devastatingly aggressive on her tiny little body that her stomach and her legs ballooned to abnormal size. The effect was that both of her legs were constantly discharging a clear fluid. It made it extremely difficult to keep her dry and comfortable. I remember with such clarity desperately trying to wipe away the liquid, but to me it was beautiful. You see, Courage hardly ever cried, and to me, when I was desperately trying to wipe away the liquid from her legs, it was as if Courage's whole body was weeping, every single pore, and I was frantically trying to wipe all those tears away. Sadly, it wasn't long after this that Courage passed away.

A few months later, one of the girls at work wanted to go see some psychics that were coming to town and she practically begged me to tag along. "I'm like totally terrified!" We were both laughing over that when my friend Dave the mailman popped into work with his daily delivery saying, "What's up with you girls today?"

You see, we love Dave. He is always so interested in what's going on with our lives. I guess that makes us feel special. I said, "We're going to see a psychic." He replied, "I don't know, I'm kind of on the fence about those things." A few mornings later, my co-worker and I were all prepared for our evening with the psychics when in popped my friend Dave the mailman. He said, "I picked this up off the ground. I want you to put it in your pocket, and if these psychics are for real, they should be able to guess what it is." A few hours later, my coworker and I were anxiously sitting at our table in a local pub awaiting the two psychics – a male and a female psychic. The male psychic had this big sketch pad and he sketched while the female psychic just studied you. It was really quite astonishing to see the emotion these two psychics could draw out of members of their audience.

When the night was drawing to a close, I knew I had to raise my hand, so I did ever so slightly (I don't pay 25 bucks for nothing). I could see both psychics zone in on me, and it wasn't long before I was sitting on stage between the two of them. They asked if I had someone who had recently passed, and I said yes, my friend Courage. The female psychic began anxiously studying me while the male psychic was frantically sketching. Then the female psychic said, "Your friend is desperately trying to get a message through to you… she wants to tell you…" At that moment, the male psychic turned around his sketch pad and revealed a page full of wings, butterfly wings, birds' wings and every type of wing imaginable. The female psychic at that same exact moment said, "Courage is desperately trying to tell you she has gotten her wings." Tears poured down my face, and I knew it was time to leave. I thanked the two psychics, my friend grabbed her coat and we headed out the door. Then something literally stopped me in my tracks. I remembered what my friend Dave the mailman had given me. I opened my pocket and pulled it out. My hand started trembling. There in my hand lay a 1967 penny engraved with a set of wings.

we bend the light

The Man Under The Hat

Dear Dave,

I thought I would return the favour

I am sending this letter to heaven

I wonder if you knew how much you meant to us all

Conveying your messages of joy, hope,

Our worries and sometimes our secrets

Through mail

You were God's messenger

With your own hidden agenda

How you served this duty

Interwoven through the web of our lives

Was your story.

Your route was your family

And you cared for us all so well

And so, our friendship began

For me my house and place of work

Were on your celestial list

Everyday for 14 years
At first a smile and a quick hello
Soon turned into "What's up Dave?"
And as you rung the bell at work
I still hear those words
"Good morning folks, just the mail"
I loved our chats
Of Life
And, of course, there were the treats
Chocolate!
On special occasions and
Just because you thought us special
Sickness sometimes kept me from work
A note in my mailbox to show you cared
"Hope you're feeling better soon"
Always made me feel better
Then there was your 50th birthday
I had made you an "Over-the-Hill treat bag"
And that sealed the deal
We were friends for life
I remember the time my first grandchild was soon to arrive
I had a bet he would be born on your birthday
I won!
Then there was "our" magical story
I loved sharing it at all my storytelling events.
The last time I shared it with an audience
It was a Friday
And I put a magic penny
Under a seat
When I finished the story
I shared the secret of the hidden penny
A young girl found it

Her face lit up
I said "See, the magic has found you"
Then two days later Dave
You left us all
I couldn't get out of bed
for three days
I visited with your wife
In your kitchen
We sat
And shared Dave stories
There were three windows
in your kitchen
Two of which had
hummingbird feeders
The humming birds came
And stayed
Your wife said it was always
like that
You loved the birds
It was clear they loved you
And so, my friend, with grief
I question
What divine intervention
Brought you to your final mail
destination
A stairway to heaven
Of worthy recipients
None other than celestial beings
Warranting such grace
To hear
Those words forever missed...
"Good morning folks,
Just the mail."

we held the light

What is love?
The answer lies
in the question.
Love what is. P

The Dealers

On occasion, I am requested to do a favor for a loved one. Just to give you an idea of how Patti's brain works, here is how it goes
1. Request by loved one to do a favor.
2. Your mission, should you choose to accept it....

A general plea for assistance with a broad description of immediate need for product went as follows: said loved one requires a blender because theirs has just broke, and one cannot maintain a healthy body without a healthy fruit smoothie for breakfast. I can sympathize with this view!

A blender has just appeared on PEI Buy and Sell. This blender is in my locality. Therefore, my mission is to pick up blender, exchange cash only for blender and meet at disclosed location. This disclosed location is at the Superstore parking lot by the red bins. Sounds pretty simple to me.

I head out, pull into the parking lot and discover woman standing outside her vehicle by red bins in Superstore parking lot. I say, "Do you have the stuff?" "Yes," she replied, continuing to open her coat, and revealed hand made baby booties and a story book... long pause....

Now I may not be Sherlock Holmes, but upon closer observation, I now notice that not only are we not the only ones on Tuesday afternoon at 1:15 by the Red Bins at Superstore, but as I broaden my visual range, I discover an entire black market of 50+ women exchanging cash for product.

Now at this moment I realize that I too am part of this black market! I can picture the headlines: "Dealer Bust by Red Bins." Relax, fellow

Islanders, it's much worse than you think. I suddenly feel like Liam Neesom in the final scene of "The Grey," where I land right in the wolves' den surrounded by wolves! Yeah, I know what you're all thinking, "Man, this girl has a vivid imagination!" All I could think of was "Abort! Abort! Abort mission!" For there in the parking lot by the red bins was a line of maybe 20 cars, all with 50+ year old ladies sitting, waiting patiently for their "deals" to go down!

Patti's mind goes to, "As always, should you or any of your team be caught, family and friends will disavow any knowledge of your action. This message will self destruct!" Great! I have just happened upon a black market of elderly dealers, of which I am now a part of, and all I can think of is "I'm going down — this isn't good. The police and FBI SWAT teams are going to swarm us and that's it. I will end up in the brig!"

Oh, happy day everyone!

Power cannot prevail where compassion exists because the truest form of compassion does not wish to remove power. It wishes to transform it. P

One year to the day

The mop moves back and forth over the floor
I look up, there has to be something more
Everyday is just the same
If this is life, I must be worthy of my pain
A background of movement to direct a different life
A door that opens into a new strife
One of wonder to explore
That I must not and cannot ignore.
Such a simple role
To care for the dying in this hole
Maybe I have something to offer
Something to share in this coffer
An outstretched hand that does not retreat
There is nothing to defeat
Just love to give
That is how I wish to live
Even for a day
A warm blanket for a face
Blackened with cancer
So close to death's embrace
But for a moment just to sit
At the bedside of one whose heart has quit
But power and money are aware
Of just how much people share
But please for the dying could you spare
Have you even looked into a room
And been with someone at their last breath
That you don't even know
Fuck this show

Just more pushing paper

To make you glow

While Power works at planning how to make more money

I have just realized I am not your fuckin' Honey

And when I find out your dirty little secret

And you remove me from this place so that I will keep it

This is how I spend the last day

The dying man shares how it eats away

The cancer like a bad apple

Rotten to the core

Oh, how I care even more

No, I say, you are mistaken

I have gone to the store

Brought back an apple and cut to its core

Your eyes open for their last

See what I have found

The seeds are there

And they have touched the ground.

Definition of Define: set forth the
meaning of, determine, decide.
Definition of Accept: believe,
recognize as valid, regard as true.
When considering all of humanity, one is
based on judgement, the other on love. P

Monsters

It never occurred to me
That I was a monster for you to see
Large, ugly and frightening.
Wicked, inhuman and cruel.
IMAGINARY terrifying creature.
A Demon inducing fear of physical harm
When I approach
Or get too close
Simply by my appearance or actions.
Large and strange Colossus
You demonstrate and warn
Revealing the evidence of our own moral ground
Ridding ourselves of such undesirable attributes
Of which we are bound
Deviant form
Versus the norm
Excising the monster
Reinforcing our purity
But wait
Defining the monster
Offers the illusion of absolution
After murder
After killing
Assassination
Execution
Massacre
Slaughter
And finally, Annihilation
Alternately forming the sublime
Which derives its pure terror
From inside
Looking out at YOU.

I enjoyed sitting next to this Gargoyle. I liked the fact that I could sit right beside him without fear. I wrote the "Monsters" poem because I know we can be demonized by others, but sometimes the person we demonize the most is ourselves. Believe me when I say this with all my heart: "Gargoyles do not exist." You are beautiful.

we bend the light

Nunchucks

Origin
  Non-weapon
    Two sticks linked by chain
      To thresh and separate
        A grain
          From the plant
Evolving
  For Night watch
    To warn of threats
Evolved
  Weapon
    Wielded in one hand
But can be paired
  To nun
    with blunt force
      To immobilize or disarm
        With increased speed
        and coordination
Evolution of words
  Weaponized
    Information
      Skillfully crafted
        Exploiting
          The vulnerable
          Through thought
            Effecting perceptions
          Social engineering
            Wielded in one hand

Paired to target

Cognitively hacking

Illegally possessing

The mind

Threshing the recipient

Promoting the attacker

Use visual tool

Etumos

Cognitive security

Non-weapon

To serve

Unborn wholeness

Evolution

Words

Advantageous association

Rebellious peasants

Romantic notion

Variation of a two-section staff

Wrapping chain of Etumos

around words

a deed done

action

In opposition to disarm

the opponent

And immobilize

In freestyle display

Quarantine Shield

The mind

The "Nunchucks" poem can be read start to finish and then finish to start with a different intention and different meaning.

we beld the light

The first time I encountered this magical tree, The Old Man's Face clearly appeared. His voice spoke of Truth and I wrote the poem called "Nunchucks." He is located on the property of the Princetown United Church in Malpeque, PEI. He was the second oldest tree on PEI at the time. The oldest tree on PEI was located in Victoria by the Sea. Due to Dutch Elm disease on PEI we lost our beautiful tree in Victoria by the Sea in November 2018. "The Old Man in the Tree" in Malpeque is now the oldest tree on PEI.

When a bad man strikes, he strikes with a bad hand, and therefore he is unjustified. When a good man strikes, he strikes with a good hand, and therefore he is justified. The thought is always the same, and the intent is always the same, and the result is always the same. The recipient feels the strike. P

we bend the light

Even trees bend. A walk in the woods in Malpeque PEI reveals magical, mystical trees.

The Rubber Band Theory is the
theory that everything is ten times more
elastic in the universe than previously
thought. In physics, as in life, the True
meaning of the Rubber Band Theory
primarily exists to represent Truth! P

The Seven Spotted Ladybug

She had three black spots
On each of her wings
And one on both.
Three jewels.
Three marks of existence.
Coexisting
With joy
To flowers.
Unfolding
Expanding
Her wings
For flight.
Guided by the
Cosmic law.
A further pair
Of wings
Tucked underneath
To hover.
Folding
And contracting
alighting
on a flower.
Crystalizing
The bloom.
Blossoming
Its radiance.

A visit from two little girls creates such magic! Remember — you are a star!

Dark at night
But Me so Bright
Who am I

Star
Sun
moon

liting
lietH

we bend the light

Sleep

Illuminating before I awaken
Only to disappear
Before consciousness suspends.

*If we do not understand the true meaning
to coexist, we will simply cease to exist. P*

My Dream

I made my way across the rolling hills and found myself at the edge of a large body of water. I had been here before. I could feel the sense of fear! The last time I tried to cross, I made no effort to save myself. I let the water engulf me and pull me down, but this time was different. On the other side of the large body of water were two horses: a stallion and a mare. They encouraged my crossing. I shook my head. The mare gently nuzzled the stallion, and in compliance, the stallion stepped back, and the mare moved forward and entered the water.

Her agility and strength were seemingly effortless as she crossed to my side, but I do not know why she chose her next action. The gesture so moved my heart, that I felt a tear roll down my face. In one tender movement, she bowed. It liberated my strength.

I found myself mounting her bareback, tightly wrapping her mane between my fingers. We entered the water and my head rested upon her nape. She moved through the water with ease. The water was warm, gently flowing over my body. Not once did I feel its pull downward. We united with the Stallion on the shore.

I was now cantering bareback across the fields and I understood now what it meant to bend a horse. For the mare was perfectly straight. Her suppleness as the key, bending left and right quite blissfully, without resistance to keep her rider safe from falling.

The sun was low in the sky and we followed the fence line to a barn. The barn door was awaiting our entry and had been left ajar. We entered the barn and the mare bowed once again and gently placed me in the hay. The stallion and the mare nuzzled and the two creatures sired by love and compassion gently departed.

The sunlight was entering through the cracks in the walls and the barn was full of energy and safely sheltered my rest. There were many other creatures in the barn, each at rest near dusk. It was not silent in the barn but there was a sweet harmony of quietness and peace which seemed to provide comfort and protection and soothed me to sleep. When I awoke there was a familiar aroma of home cooking. I followed the appealing aromas out of the barn. There was a cobblestone walkway leading to a large stone house. The lights were on in the house

we beld the light

and I heard someone whistling. As the barn faded into the background, I followed the walkway up to the home. The back door had been left ajar and I entered the kitchen.

There was a man who moved about quite aptly and was skillfully preparing a meal. His strong presence reassured my entrance, and I felt he was a master chef who delighted in his work.

A woman was busily setting the table and had made three place settings. The man and the woman nodded cheerfully and acknowledged my presence as I sat down at their table. The food smelled so good and in anticipation my mouth began to water.

The man came and delivered the meal to the table delighting my appetite. He then sat and patiently waited. I watched the woman take my plate and begin to serve the meal, bending right, then left with such grace. The suppleness of her gentle nature seemed familiar and then I knew. Sired by love and compassion, a meal was prepared for me. There was no resistance on this path. I bowed my head and gave thanks for the blessing, which nourished my body and refreshed my soul.

we held the light

Very old and sacred trees exist everywhere in the world. I believe they are all connected through their roots. We are most fortunate on our gentle Island to have a sacred tree. If you ever get the chance to talk to "The Old Man in the Tree," I hope he whispers "Magic" in your ear. I like to believe that compassion exists within all of us, and it is the root of all peace on this earth with its branches extending outwards, embracing the sun.

Achelois

The oracle stated
Her delicate gender
Would be the intermediary between
People and the divine
A quest
Of just cause
For the moon goddess
She who washes away pain
Conceding descent
For a goddess cannot exist in reality
She was simply the rain
A feeling
Relinquishing pain
But maybe that was the key
Her wounds open
A water nymph
Of tears
A residual token
Of ownership
With bended knee
Leaning in towards
Her humanity
Honoring all beings
Hovering
A droplet
Surrendering to
its origin
only visible
for contact
a kerchief
to your domain.

Copernicus revealed the paradigm shift...our
Earth revolving around the sun... But each
human being has its own Ptolemaic model con-
ditioned into its perspectives throughout the ages
of their time...the human a constant expecting
the sun to move...rising and setting according to
their day...In reality the sun awaits our arrival...
P

we bend the light

Patti Arsenault lives in Summerside, Prince Edward Island with her husband Keith and their dog Max. She believes that Magic exists everywhere in the funny moments, the sad and the profound. Sharing her enchanting delightful world of "PEI" with its irresistible charm to friends from everywhere has been a lifelong dream of hers. From captivating sold out audiences at MoMonday's in Halifax, to Chautauqua, CBC Spin Time, live radio dramas, guest speaking at various schools, and Storytelling in Malpeque, she hopes you find your way to this magical, mystical place she calls "Home"!